T0349165

## MODERN HERALDRY: VOLUME 1

'Modern Heraldry' is our attempt to bring together a profusely illustrated guide to more than 350 trademarks, based on heraldic symbology, from all over the world.

As part of Counter-Print's wide survey of logo design, the starting point for this title was the observation that many present day marks still draw upon traditional symbols such as the heraldic mark or logos that share its characteristics.

The heraldic mark is widely used and although it occasionally derives from the founder's family crest, it is more commonly used in an attempt to convey a sense of respectability for a commercial venture. The treatment is either seen as a byword for dignity and dependability or perhaps a subversive tactic when establishing a modern identity.

The trademark designs in this book are grouped under category headings chosen for their heraldic connotations. The categories included are: shields, crests, stamps, seals, laurels, flags and crowns.

We have not attempted to show every major designer's work or to give equal coverage by country. Many of the logos are by young designers and are reproduced for the first time.

We would like to thank the designers and owners of the trademarks who have contributed material and information for this book.

**Jon Dowllng**
Counter-Print

1

2

3

4

5

6

**1. Pelican's Nest**
Restaurant & bar
USA
J Fletcher Design
jfletcherdesign.com
2014

**2. Gemeinde Vechigen**
Municipality
Switzerland
Atelier Bundi AG
atelierbundi.ch
2013

**3. The Snug**
Digital agency
USA
Salih Kucukaga Design Studio
salihkucukaga.com
2015

**4. Brooklyn Nets**
Self-initiated
USA
DCL
derrickclee.com
2012

**5. Crea Cultura**
Organisation dedicated to
promoting art and culture
through artistic residences,
and supporting research
and the development of
dialogue & coexistence
between artists of different
nationalities
Spain
Erretres
erretres.com
2013

**6. Gemeinde Köniz**
Municipality
Switzerland
Atelier Bundi AG
atelierbundi.ch
1990

**7. Bikaramba**
Guided bicycle tours
Canada
Doublenaut
doublenaut.com
2013

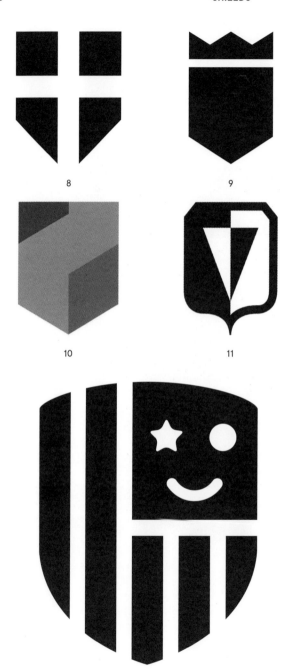

8

9

10

11

12

**13. Holy Family University**
Educational institution
USA
Taylor Design
taylordesign.com
2012

**14. Município de Alenquer**
Public administration
Portugal
Miguel Palmeiro Designer
miguelpalmeiro.com
2012

13

14

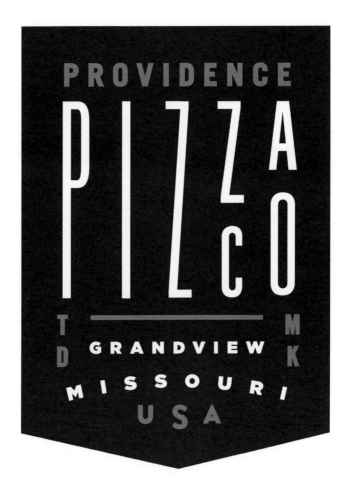

**15. Providence Pizza**
Pizza restaurant
USA
Foundry Collective
foundryco.com
2014

**16. Getaways NYC**
Bicycle & apparel lifestyle brand
USA
J Fletcher Design
jfletcherdesign.com
2014

17

18

19

20

**17. North Standard Trading Post**
Clothing & lifestyle shop
Canada
Doublenaut
doublenaut.com
2013

**18. Rutledge Cab Co.**
Restaurant & bar
USA
J Fletcher Design
jfletcherdesign.com
2013

**19. Victoria Small Business Catalyst**
A venture capital organisation
for local businesses
Canada
Riley Cran
rileycran.com
2013

**20. The Longboard**
Restaurant & bar
USA
J Fletcher Design
jfletcherdesign.com
2014

**21. Heineken**
Dutch brewing company
USA
High Tide
hightide.nyc
2013

**22. Porter House**
Vegan fare & fine ales
Canada
Doublenaut
doublenaut.com
2014

**23. The Championship
of Lady Arm Wrestlers**
A non-profit that puts on arm
wrestling events for charity
USA
Convoy
weareconvoy.com
2012

**24. Nike**
Multinational footwear
& apparel brand
USA
High Tide
hightide.nyc
2010

22

23

25

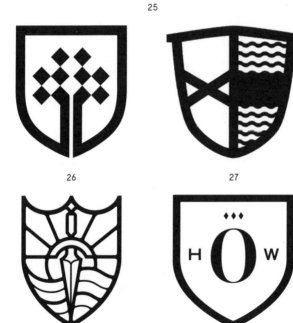

26       27

28       29

**25. The Union of Architects of Montenegro**
Union of architects
Montenegro
Maksim Arbuzov
maksimarbuzov.com
2010

**26. Dr. B L Kapur Super Speciality Hospital**
Hospital
India
Alok Nanda & Company
aloknanda.com
1959

**27. Shilling Bier – Uli Bacher**
Beer brewer &
restaurant owner
Austria
moodley brand identity
moodley.at
2014

**28. Citizen**
Micro brewery
South Africa
Monday Design
mondaydesign.co.za
2012

**29. Oliver Building for McKnight Realty Partners**
Real estate investment
& development company
USA
Yossi Belkin
yossigraphicdesign.com
2013

**30. Time Out Sports**
Sporting goods
USA
J Fletcher Design
Jfletcherdesign.com
2013

**31. Boogüd**
Builders of bicycles made
from recycled bamboo
USA
Travis Ladue
travisladue.com
2012

**32. De Wouwse Plantage**
Real estate & golf
Netherlands
Boy Bastiaens/StormHand
stormhand.com
2014

30

31

33

34

35

36

•••

37

38

39

40

**33. Villa Maria**
Educational institution
USA
Taylor Design
taylordesign.com
2010

**34. Creative Treachery**
Clothing brand
USA
CAP.388
cap.388.com
2014

**35. Bobbi Brown**
Cosmetics
USA
Ian Brignell Lettering Design
ianbrignell.com
2007

**36. Betsy Smith Worldwide**
Copywriting & consulting
USA
Eight Hour Day
eighthourday.com
2010

**37. The Rickety Press**
Public house & bar
United Kingdom
Ged Palmer
gedpalmer.com
2012

**38. El Aristo**
Tea company
Argentina
empatía®
helloempatia.com
2014

**39. Lantana**
Boutique hotel
USA
Slaughter Group
slaughtergroup.com

**40. Hallman Hill**
Real estate development
USA
Slaughter Group
slaughtergroup.com

**41. Clifton Arms Hotel**
Hotel, restaurant, bar & brasserie
United Kingdom
Wash Design Studio
wash-design.co.uk
2012

**42. Kolståhl**
Stationery manufacturers
USA
Studio Weidemüller
weidemuller.com
2014

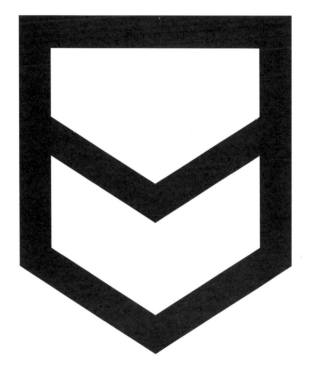

**43. Vrijmoed**
Restaurant
Belgium
Chilli
chilli.be
2014

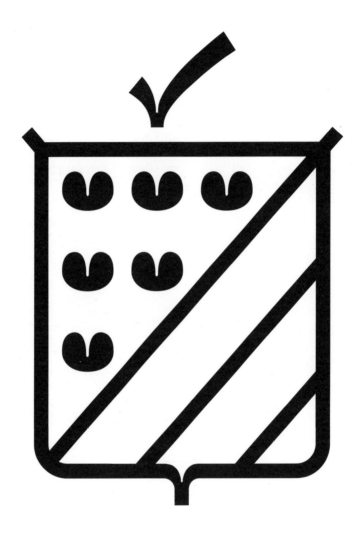

**44. Checklist**
Custom event planning
Mexico
Anagrama
anagrama.com
2013

**45. Moriitalia**
Homeware
Vietnam
Design Positive
design-positive.com
2010

**46. AUSTRAL**
Clothing
Spain
Los Kennedy
loskennedy.com
2012

**47. Bullman Security**
Residential home security
& maintenance
USA
John McHugh
johnmchugh.net
2012

**48. FR Solutions**
Provides fire resistant
solutions
Poland
Motyf Studio
motyfstudio.com
2014

**49. Bench**
Financial services startup
Canada
Roger Dario
rogerdario.com
2012

**50. JF Legal**
Law firm
Poland
Dmowski & Co.
dmowski.co
2014

**51. Atypical**
Handmade cruisers producer
Italy
Think Work Observe
t-wo.it
2012

45      46

47

48      49

50      51

**52. Major League Soccer**
U.S soccer league
USA
Athletics
athleticsnyc.com
1993

**53. Rivalswag**
College merchandise company
USA
CAP.388
cap388.com
2013

54                            55

56

57                            58

**54. Triumph & Disaster**
Skin & hair products
New Zealand
DD/MM/YY
ddmmyy.com
2011

**55. South Cowichan Lawn
Tennis Club**
Tennis club
Canada
dngSTUDIO
dngstudio.com

**56. Ashford & Ashford**
Lawyer specialising in oil
field property rights
USA
Ghost
ghostokc.com
2012

**57. Valle Agredo —
Unione dei Comuni del
Camposampierese**
Union of municipalities
Italy
Tankboys
tankboys.biz
2013

**58. Pachtloket**
Juridical advice
Belgium
Chilli
chilli.be
2015

**59. Pacific Rim**
Currency exchange
Canada
dngSTUDIO for
Taiji Brand Group
dngstudio.com
2008

**60. The Groom**
Horses & riding
Belgium
Chilli
chilli.be
2014

**61. McKenzie Law Firm**
Law firm
USA
idgroup
idgroupbranding.com
2014

**62. Precept**
Self-initated
United Kingdom
Precept
precept.co.uk
2010

**63. Cox Auto**
Automotive service centre
Australia
Pennant
studiopennant.com
2014

59

60

61

62

63

**64. San Javier City Council**
Administration, government
& public services
Spain
Jose Carratala
behance.net/joseignaciocarratala
2013

**65. Maria Rigol Ordi**
Winery & cellar
Spain
Atipus
atipus.com
2013

**66. Pacharán**
Basque tavern
Uruguay
Mundial
mundial.uy
2014

**67. Cicada Books**
Publisher
United Kingdom
April
studio-april.com
2015

**68. Harrison Limited**
Men's clothing
USA
Slaughter Group
slaughtergroup.com

**69. Monocle**
Global affairs & lifestyle
magazine
United Kingdom
Ty Wilkins
tywilkins.com
2013

65

66

67

68

69

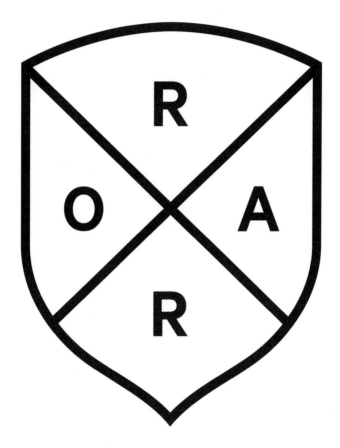

**70. Roar Projects**
Hospitality holding company
Australia
Principle Design
principledesign.com.au
2013

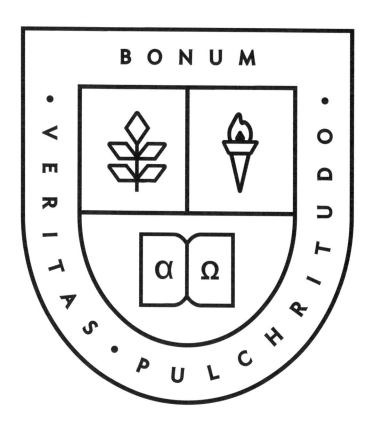

**71. Instituto de Humanidades
Francesco Petrarca**
Francesco Petrarca Liberal
Arts School
Spain
Nueve Estudio
n-u-e-v-e.com
2013

**72. Urban Group**
Property developer
Taiwan, China
Studio Weidemüller
weidemuller.com
2015

**73. Fundación Deporte Galego**
Sport events & promotion
Spain
Tres Tipos Gráficos
trestiposgraficos.com
2011

72

73

**74. Verseidag Ballistic Protection**
Armour products
Finland
Werklig
werklig.com
2013

**75. MY Construction**
International construction
Turkey
Deney Design Studio
deney.com.tr
2009

**76. Cloud Compliance Corporation**
Business compliance checks
United Kingdom
I See Sea
iseesea.co.uk
2014

**77. Plugged In PR**
Music PR
United Kingdom
I See Sea
iseesea.co.uk
2014

**78. Cosure**
Insurance
Belgium
Chilli
chilli.be
2011

**79. Route 11**
Dance festival
USA
Convoy
weareconvoy.com
2014

**80. Caravan**
Restaurant, bar & roastery
United Kingdom
Inhouse
inhouse.nz
2010

**81. Bakery & Gourmet**
Restaurant
Brazil
P/P Studio
pedropaulino.com
2013

74

75

76

77

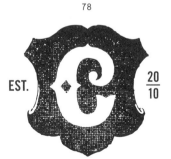

78

79

80

81

# Via Italia

*Budapest*

**82. Via Italia Budapest**
Italian street in Budapest
Italy & Hungary
Kissmiklos
kissmiklos.com
2015

83                                        84

85                                        86

87

**83. The Cake Shop**
Bespoke cakes
United Kingdom
Smiling Wolf
smilingwolf.co.uk
2014

**84. Haven & Havok**
Clothing company
USA
CAP.388
cap388.com
2013

**85. Ticiane Pinheiro**
Actress & model
Brazil
P/P Studio
pedropaulino.com
2012

**86. Luppolo Pizzeria**
Bar & restaurant
United Kingdom
Mr Gresty (Studio)
mrgresty.com
2014

**87. Manifest Digital**
Interactive design
& development
USA
Eight Hour Day
eighthourday.com
2011

**88. Esquire**
Magazine
USA
Mikey Burton
mikeyburton.com
2013

**89. Esquire**
Magazine
USA
Mikey Burton
mikeyburton.com
2013

**90. Esquire**
Magazine
USA
Mikey Burton
mikeyburton.com
2013

**91. Esquire**
Magazine
USA
Mikey Burton
mikeyburton.com
2013

**92. Work & Play**
Clothing company
Denmark
BRUNSWICKER studio
brunswicker.dk
2010

88

89

90

91

92

93

94

95

96

97

**93. Blog Society
(part of Telegraaf Media Group)**
Blog Society connects
the best Dutch blogs
& social media fanatics in
an exclusive community
Netherlands
Evers + de Gier
eversendegier.nl
2014

**94. Puma**
Sportswear
Germany
Golden Gate
thegoldengate.eu
2013

**95. The Cub Reporter**
Newspaper
USA
Trevor Rogers
trevorgrogers.com
2014

**96. Nata da Nata**
Food & beverage
Portugal
Miguel Palmeiro Designer
miguelpalmeiro.com
2014

**97. Swords For Hire**
Self-initiated
USA
Greg Christman Design
gregchristmandesign.com
2014

**98. Social HQ**
Workspace
United Kingdom
Precept
precept.co.uk
2011

99

100

101

102

**99. Bird Apartment Printing**
Screen printing company
USA
Greg Christman Design
gregchristmandesign.com
2012

**100. Function**
Coffee roaster
USA
Salih Kucukaga Design Studio
salihkucukaga.com
2014

**101. Pastatore**
Pasta manufacturer
Germany
Glenn Garriock
garriock.com
2014

**102. Rise and Shine Paper**
Letterpress company
USA
Greg Christman Design
gregchristmandesign.com
2013

**103. The Greater Seattle
Bureau of Fearless Ideas**
Non-profit writing & tutoring
center for young people
ages 6 to 18
USA
Spencer Charles
spencercharles.com
2014

103

104. Southbank Employers Group
Culture & tourism
United Kingdom
IWANT
iwantdesign.com
2013

**105. Rotary Klubi**
Night club
Estonia
AKU
aku.co
2009

**106. Camp and Furnace**
Restaurant, bar, fanpark,
conference venue & cultural
hangout
United Kingdom
Smiling Wolf
smilingwolf.co.uk
2012

105

106

**107. Browton's**
Craft beer shop
United Kingdom
Loose Collective
studioloose.co.uk
2014

**108. Browton's**
Craft beer shop
United Kingdom
Loose Collective
studioloose.co.uk
2014

**109. Browton's**
Craft beer shop
United Kingdom
Loose Collective
studioloose.co.uk
2014

**110. Dream Clothing/**
**Hakeem Olajuwon**
Fashion
USA
Salih Kucukaga Design Studio
salihkucukaga.com
2012

**111. Fabrikk**
Restaurant
Turkey
Salih Kucukaga Design Studio
salihkucukaga.com
2010

107

108

109

110

111

**112. Agriart Ifjúsági, Zenei
és Kulturális Egyesület**
Youth culture association
Hungary
Ilkka Janatuinen
ilkkaj.com
2013

113

114

**113. Baku Maeda**
Art project
Japan
COMMUNE
commune-inc.jp
2010

**114. Atelier LaDurance**
Denim goods
Netherlands
Boy Bastiaens/StormHand
stormhand.com
2005

**115. Coffee House London**
Coffee house
United Kingdom
Reynolds and Reyner
reynoldsandreyner.com
2005

115

116

117

118            119

120            121

122

**118. Junta de Extremadura**
Government of
Extremadura region
Spain
Cruz Novillo
cruznovillo.com
1978

**119. Onkja**
Produces unique clothes
and accessories for children
& mothers
Netherlands
Motyf Studio
motyfstudio.com
2013

**120. Quinto Centenario del
Descubrimiento de America**
500th anniversary of the
discovery of America
Spain
Cruz Novillo
cruznovillo.com
1981

**121. Cuerpo Nacional
de Policia**
Spanish national police
Spain
Cruz Novillo
cruznovillo.com
1986

**122. Correos**
Spanish postal service
Spain
Cruz Novillo
cruznovillo.com
1977

**123. Lowbrau**
Restaurant
USA
Mode Design (Hans Bennewitz)
modedesign.us
2012

**124. Real Madrid**
Foundation of Real Madrid
football club
Spain
Cruz Novillo
cruznovillo.com
1991

123

124

125                    126

**125. Kronan Trademark AB**
Manufacturer of bicycles,
prams & pushchairs
Sweden
Ateljé Altmann
ateljealtmann.com
2011

**126. Banco Industrial
de Leon**
Industrial Bank of Leon
Spain
Cruz Novillo
cruznovillo.com
1972

**127. Duchy Originals**
Organic food
United Kingdom
Rob Clarke Type Design
& Lettering/LRW Design
robclarke.com
2008

127

**128. Comunidad de Madrid**
Community of Madrid
Spain
Cruz Novillo
cruznovillo.com
1984

129

130

**129. Royal Mail Rethink
for ICON Magazine**
Magazine
United Kingdom
Mash Creative
mashcreative.co.uk
2011

**130. Crowns Guides/
Zeitgeist Books**
Publisher
USA
Hazen Creative, Inc.
hazencreative.com
2004

**131. Scottish Parliament**
National parliament
United Kingdom
Peter Horridge
horridge.com
1999

131

**132. Marquette University**
Higher education
USA & Italy
Jack Muldowney Design Co.
jackmuldowney.com
2010

**133. Vicky Cristina Tapas Bar**
Tapas bar
Israel
kissmiklos
kissmiklos.com
2015

**134. Gieves & Hawkes**
Savile row tailor
United Kingdom
StudioSmall
studiosmall.com
2009

CAGLI 2010
MARQUETTE

132          133

1771
No1 SAVILE ROW

134

**135. The Royal Danish Academy of Fine Arts**
Creative institution of higher education
Denmark
Studio Daniel Siim
danielsiim.dk
2011

**136. Prince Ink Co.**
Premium print maker
& screen printing
USA
The BlkSmith Co.
theblksmith.com
2014

135

136

**137. Royal Braun**
Content consultancy
& search firm
USA
DIA
dia.tv
2014

**138. Taylor Black**
Jewellery
United Kingdom
Interabang
interabang.uk.com
2011

**139. Anna Lou of London**
Jewellery & accessories
United Kingdom
Burobraak
burobraak.nl
2012

**140. Storybird Inc.**
Visual publishing platform
USA & Canada
Sam Dallyn
samdallyn.co.uk
2014

137

138

139

140

SUPREME **BRITISH** PROTEIN

# KINGS
## BILTONG™

**141. Kings Bilton**
High protein snacks
United Kingdom
Robot Food Ltd
robot-food.com
2013

**142. AdSoup**
Digital marketing
United Kingdom
I See Sea
iseesea.co.uk
2013

**143. Alessandro Ripellino Arkitekter/Järngrinden**
Architect & building construction
Sweden
BankerWessel
bankerwessel.com
2014

**144. OLIO E OSS**
Skincare products
USA
AfterAll Studio
afterallstudio.com
2012

**145. Victoria Ruiz**
Makers of high quality wood doors
Mexico
Firmalt
firmalt.com
2013

**146. Capitol Couture**
Fashion blog
USA
P/P Studio
pedropaulino.com
2013

**147. What Matters Most**
Creative studio
Netherlands
High Tide
hightide.nyc
2009

**148. Fernando Torres**
Photographer
Spain
Jorge León
leonjorge.com
2013

**149. Parkham Living**
Lifestyle blog
USA
Mode Design
(Hans Bennewitz)
modedesign.us
2014

**150. Paris Boutique**
Dress house
United Kingdom
Precept
precept.co.uk
2013

143

144

146

145

148

149

150

151

152

153

154

155

**151. Prosjektklubben (The Project Club)**
Multi-disiplinary club including photography, motion, illustration, graphic design, web design & programming
Norway
Jon Arne Berg (with help and direction from Jonas Bødtker & Nils Skogstrøm)
jonarneberg.no
2011

**152. Firenze&Fashion for RCS Periodici**
Fashion night for a publisher
Italy
Kuchar Swara
kucharswara.com
2011

**153. B|D Landscape Architects**
Landscape architects
United Kingdom
Passport
wearepassport.com
2014

**154. Merchandwise**
Promotional solutions
Uruguay
Mundial
mundial.uy
2012

**155. Pilgrim**
Jewellery
Denmark
Homework
homework.dk
2014

**156. Herbert Parkinson**
One of the few remaining
textile manufacturers In
Britain, producing a range
of products which are sold
in John Lewis
United Kingdom
Charlie Smith Design
charliesmithdesign.com
2013

**157. World Cup Stamps**
Self-initiated
Portugal
MAAN Design Studio
maandesign.com
2014

**158. Curation Guild
Printing Co.**
Printing company
Denmark
CAP.388
cap388.com
2014

**159. Catholic League
Champions**
Boutique media
& promotions firm
USA
Jack Muldowney
Design Co.
jackmuldowney.com
2014

**160. 18° Cartório**
Registry of notes
Brazil
P/P Studio
pedropaulino.com
2012

156

157

158

159

160

161

162

163

164

165

**161. Spanish Armada**
Promotion of Spanish
culture in the United
Kingdom
Spain
Los Kennedy
loskennedy.com
2013

**162. Danmarks
Rederiforening/Danish
Shipowners' Association**
Trade and employer
organisation for shipowners
& offshore companies
Denmark
Designbolaget
designbolaget.dk
2011

**163. Monday Delight**
A curated healthy snack
delivery service
USA
Jack Muldowney
Design Co.
jackmuldowney.com
2012

**164. Malene Birger**
Interior decorating
Denmark
Homework
homework.dk
2012

**165. Scarinish**
Architecture & interiors
United Kingdom
KVGD
kerrvernon.co.uk
2014

**166. Dos Santos**
Taco restaurant
USA
Mast, in collaboration
with Scott Hill
studiomast.co
2014

**167. Back To Basics**
Online design journal
Ireland
Duane Dalton
duanedalton.com
2013

**168. Scientific People**
Recruitment consultancy
for the scientific sector
United Kingdom
KVGD
kerrvernon.co.uk
2013

**169. Eastern Trading**
Wine merchant
Mauritius
Monday Design
mondaydesign.co.za
2012

**170. Deep Search**
Clothing & shoe label
Norway
Bielke+Yang
bielkeyang.com
2011

166     167

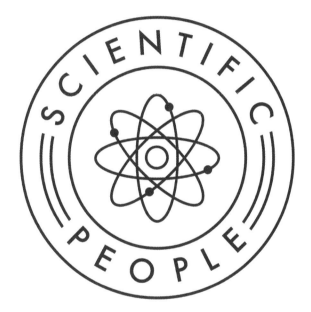

168

169     170

171

172

173

174

175

**176. Mazetti**
Chocolate factory
Sweden
Olle Eksell
olleeksell.se
1958

**177. Wunderpass**
Travel
Australia
Salih Kucukaga Studio
salihkucukaga.com
2014

**178. Alex & Martin**
Child's baptism
Spain
CAP.388
cap388.com
2014

**179. Good Vibes Café**
Café
United Kingdom
I See Sea
iseesea.co.uk
2015

**180. Ediciones Daga**
Publisher
Chile
Sebastián Rodríguez Besa
sebastianrodriguez.ch
Year 2010

176

177

178

179

180

**181. W.B.Samson**
Bakery
Norway
Work
work.no
2008

**182. Dimitre Electric Co.**
Lighting
USA
Anthony Dimitre
anthonydimitre.com
2014

183

184

185

186

187

188

189

190

**183. Bare Tea Co.**
Tea
USA
Salih Kucukaga
Studio
salihkucukaga.com
2015

**184. Vitae Spirits Distillery**
Distillery & tasting room
USA
Convoy
weareconvoy.com
2015

**185. Seaside**
New urbanist community
USA
Slaughter Group
slaughtergroup.com

**186. Luna de Oriente
for Marta Briseño
& Scott Cole**
Medical centre
Mexico & USA
Estudio Menta
estudiomenta.mx
2014

**187. The Northern Post**
Editorial
USA
Forest
thisisforest.com
2012

**188. Tooth Brothers**
Dental office
New Zealand
Mike Collinge
mikecollinge.com
2012

**189. Locl**
High-end surfer apparel
USA
High Tide
hightide.nyc
2014

**190. Park National**
Creative agency
Canada
Michael Mason
mmason.ca
2013

**191. City and Colour**
Musician
Canada
Doublenaut
doublenaut.com
2014

**192. Fornebu S**
Shopping centre
Norway
Work
work.no
2013

**193. Sogga**
Shoe company
Mexico
empatía®
helloempatia.com
2014

**194. Amigos Skate Shop**
Skate shop
Spain
Jorge León & Iris Tarraga
leonjorge.com
iristarraga.com
2014

**195. Breyburn**
Luxury menswear
USA
High Tide
hightide.nyc
2012

194

195

**196. Long Barn**
Retail
United Kingdom
Irving & Co
irvingandco.com
2010

**197. Camp and Furnace**
Restaurant, bar, fanpark,
conference venue
& cultural hangout
United Kingdom
Smiling Wolf
smilingwolf.co.uk
2012

**198. Husky Rescue/
El Camino Records**
Musical artist
& record label
Finland
Tsto
tsto.org
2011

**199. Oficina Tato**
Furniture
Brazil
P/P Studio
pedropaulino.com
2014

**200. Harlem Gourmet**
Food import company
Norway
Work
work.no
2008

196                                     197

198                                     199

200

**201. Printed and Co.**
Bespoke fabric printing
United Kingdom
KVGD
kerrvernon.co.uk
2014

**202. Retro Living**
Mid-century furniture,
art & lighting retailer
United Kingdom
Bostock and Pollitt
bostockandpollitt.com
2013

**203. Juice Warrior**
Cold-pressed juice company
United Kingdom
KVGD
kerrvernon.co.uk
2014

**204. Fanie Van Zyl**
Industrial design
South Africa
Monday Design
mondaydesign.co.za
2013

205

206

207

208

209

**205. Pulse Production**
Film & production company
USA
Simon Walker
simonwalkertype.com
2014

**206. Fraser Academy**
Private school for children
with language-based
learning disabilities
Canada
Nancy Wu Design
nancywudesign.com
2013

**207. Pacific Electric
Picture Co.**
Actor Ed Helms' production
company
USA
Simon Walker
simonwalkertype.com
2013

**208. Hot Italian**
Pizza restaurant
USA
Mode Design (Hans
Bennewitz) while at
Fuel Creative Group
modedesign.us
fuelcreativegroup.com
2013

**209. James Wylde & Co.**
French scenic wallpaper
USA
Naauao
naauao.com
2015

**210. Jamestown Revival**
Band from Austin, Texas
USA
Simon Walker
simonwalkertype.com
2013

**211. The Bread Factory**
Bakery
United Kingdom
Charlie Smith Design
charliesmithdesign.com
2014

**212. Stonewood Farm**
Farm
USA
Louise Fili Ltd
louisefili.com
2014

**213. Isle of Mull Scallops**
Supplies fresh Scottish
west coast scallops
United Kingdom
my:creative
thisismycreative.com
2011

**214. Spori.com**
Website
Turkey
Salih Kucukaga Design
Studio
salihkucukaga.com
2013

210

211

213

212

214

**215. Half & Half**
Coffee shop
USA
Chris Allen
cp-allen.com
2014

**216. Scotch & Iron**
Clothing company
USA
David Gutiérrez
cargocollective.com/
davidgtz
2012

215

216

217

218

**219. No. Six Depot**
Coffee roaster & café
USA
Perky Brothers
perkybros.com
2013

**220. Stone Way Cafe**
Coffee, food & music
USA
Shore
madebyshore.com
2014

SIX
No
DEPOT

219

STONE
WAY
CAFE

220

**221. Eat Chocolates Artesanals**
Handmade chocolates
Brazil
P/P Studio
pedropaulino.com
2013

**222. Arkade Clothing Company**
Clothing company
USA
David Gutiérrez
cargocollective.com/
davidgtz
2013

**223. Hunajainen SAM (25 Year Anniversary Emblem)**
Honey production, importing & product development of honey-based products
Finland
Werklig
werklig.com
2011

**224. Sagrante**
Hibiscus liqueur
Mexico
Parallel
byparallel.com
2015

**225. Secret Nature**
Herbal tea blends
Israel
Dan Alexander & Co
daitd.com
2011

221

222

223

224

225

**226. El Cercle Restaurant**
Restaurant
Spain
Albert Romagosa
Cabinet
albertromagosa.com
2014

**227. Hansandfranz**
Industrial design studio
Germany
Golden Gate
thegoldengate.eu
2013

226

227

**228. Fanie Van Zyl**
Industrial design
South Africa
Monday Design
mondaydesign.co.za
2013

**229. LUTHIA**
Backpacks & totes
Argentina
empatia®
helloempatia.com
2014

FANIE VAN ZYL STUDIO

228

BACKPACKS & TOTES · SINCE 2012 ·

229

**230. Hopa Studio**
Self-initiated
Poland
Hopa Studio
hopastudio.com
2014

**231. Agathe Jacquillat**
Logo for Agathe Jacquillat's limited
edition artist prints she creates for
FL@33's sister-company Stereohype
France & Austria
FL@33
flat33.com
2014

AVOKONTTORIAVOKONTTORI

*(cupcake icon)*

232

AVOKONTTORIAVOKONTTORI

*(coffee cup icon)*

233

**232. Avokonttori**
Public workspace
& coffee bar
Finland
Schick Toikka
schick-toikka.com
2012

**233. Avokonttori**
Public workspace
& coffee bar
Finland
Schick Toikka
schick-toikka.com
2012

234

235

236

237

238

239

**236. Los Italianos**
Italian traditional food
company from Piamonte,
established in Barcelona
since 1939
Italy
Huaman Studio
huamanstudio.com
2014

**237. Juice Served Here**
A raw, organic cold-pressed
juice company
USA
Hype Type Studio
hypetype.co.uk
2013

**238. Bodega Barcelona**
Provides & sells Spanish
drinks in the USA
USA
Firma
firma.es
2014

**239. Food Studio**
Hosting of dinners, seminars,
catering, talks, foraging etc
Norway
Bielke+Yang
bielkeyang.com
2012

**240. Artisan Biscuits**
Handmade biscuits
United Kingdom
Rob Clarke Type Design
& Lettering/Irving & Co
robclarke.com
2007

**241. Lady & Maker**
Small goods designer
USA
Travis Ladue
travisladue.com
2014

**242. Central Standard**
**Brewing**
Brewery
USA
Simon Walker
simonwalkertype.com
2014

241

242

ONE
ROASTER
ONE
QUALITY
HAND CRAFTED

243

244

245

246

247

**248. Boeuf & Bun**
Gourmet burger restaurant
USA
Yossi Belkin
yossigraphicdesign.com
2014

**249. The South Range**
Self-initiated
USA
Simon Walker
simonwalkertype.com
2014

**250. Stark Raving Whiskey**
Hand-crafted Tennessee
whiskey
USA
Hype Type Studio
hypetype.co.uk
2014

248

249

250

# EMBASSY

### OF
### BRICKS AND LOGS

**251. Embassy of Bricks and Logs**
Streetwear shop
Germany
Golden Gate
thegoldengate.eu
2011

**252. Ludwig Reiter**
Shoemaker
Austria
Golden Gate, commissioned
by Anzinger Wuenschner Rasp
thegoldengate.eu
2008

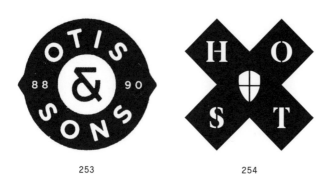

253                           254

**253. Otis & Sons**
Lifestyle household goods
& decor
USA
The BlkSmith Co.
theblksmith.com
2013

**254. Host**
Advertising agency
Australia
Design by Toko
designbytoko.com
2011

**255. Articulate**
E-Learning software
USA
Greg Christman Design
gregchristmandesign.com
2015

255

**256. Cutty Sark**
Culture & tourism destination
United Kingdom
IWANT
iwantdesign.com
2014

**257. Las Cabras**
Restaurant
Chile
Sebastián Rodríguez Besa
sebastianrodriguez.ch
2014

**258. J.P. Graziano Grocery
& Sub Shop**
Family-owned Italian grocer
USA
Jack Muldowney Design Co.
jackmuldowney.com
2014

**259. Helen Keller Institute**
Foundation
USA
Slaughter Group
slaughtergroup.com

**260. The Henry for Spirit
Investments**
Real estate development
USA
The Working Assembly
theworkingassembly.com
2015

**261. Scotland Can Make It!
for Panel**
Stamp to mark souvenirs
for the 'Scotland Can
Make It!' exhibition
United Kingdom
Graphical House
graphicalhouse.com
2012

**262. LuxDeLux**
Interior design
United Kingdom
kissmiklos
kissmiklos.com
2012

**263. Charlotte Stone**
Women's shoes
USA
AfterAll Studio
afterallstudio.com
2012

256

257

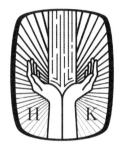

258

259

260

261

262

263

**264. Rachel Carley Ceramics**
Ceramicist
New Zealand
Inhouse
inhouse.nz
2014

**265. The National Trust –
Coughton Court**
Historic building
& destination
United Kingdom
IWANT
iwantdesign.com
2015

**266. Kute Cake**
Cupcake manufacturer
United Kingdom
IWANT
iwantdesign.com
2015

**267. Boot**
Restaurant
USA
Forest
thisisforest.com
2010

**268. Octaevo**
High-end products
for the desk & home
Spain
Studio Marcel Baer
marcel-baer.com
2013

264

265

266

267

268

**269. Finnish Cultural Institute for the Benelux (Pekka of Finland Exhibition)**
The Finnish Cultural Institute for the Benelux acts as a link between cultural stakeholders in Finland & the Benelux countries
Finland & Belgium
Werklig
werklig.com
2011

**270. Dinner Club**
Monthly dinner gatherings
USA
Naauao
naauao.com
2014

**271. Highland House**
Real estate development
Canada
Nancy Wu Design & Free Agency Creative
nancywudesign.com
freeagencycreative.com
2011

**272. Six Mile Bridge**
Micro brewery
USA
Monday Design
mondaydesign.co.za
2015

269

270

271

272

**273. Espresso Republic**
Coffee roaster
USA
Salih Kucukaga Studio
salihkucukaga.com
2011

**274. Coppi**
Restaurant
United Kingdom
Rob Clarke Type Design
& Lettering/Hamill Bosket
Dempsey
robclarke.com
2013

**275. Three Double-0 9
for Heb**
Restaurant
USA
Simon Walker
simonwalkertype.com
2014

**276. Authentic Photo**
Photography
USA
Riley Cran
rileycran.com
2013

273

274

275

276

**277. No-Li Brewhouse**
Craft brewery
USA
Riley Cran
rileycran.com
2014

**278. Brooklyn General Store**
Craft store
USA
Kelly Thorn
kellythorn.com
2014

277

278

279

280

281

282

283

284

**279. Articulate**
E-Learning software
USA
Greg Christman Design
gregchristmandesign.com
2015

**280. Vulcano Derby Girls**
Roller derby team
Spain
Eduardo Dosuá
eduardodosua.com
2014

**281. Greencity Wholefoods**
Wholefoods supplier
United Kingdom
KVGD
kerrvernon.co.uk
2013

**282. Burger Station**
Chain of burger restaurants
Spain
Nueve Estudio
n-u-e-v-e.com
2014

**283. Imbue**
Bespoke furniture
Ireland
Duane Dalton
duanedalton.com
2014

**284. Helsinki Food Company**
Design & production services
for the food industry
Finland
Werklig
werklig.com
2012

**285. Destroy Co.**
Footwear manufacturers
USA
CAP.388
cap388.com
2012

**286. Habanero Film Sales
for Alfredo Calvino**
Distribution company based
in Brazil that represents &
promotes the work of Latin
American filmmakers
Cuba
Estudio Menta
estudiomenta.mx
2014

**287. Shamrock Food
Concepts**
A Metro Detroit catering
company with focus on high
quality ingredients
USA
Jack Muldowney Design Co.
jackmuldowney.com
2010

**288. High Tide**
Self-initiated
USA
High Tide
hightide.nyc
2014

285

286

287

288

**289. Goldzahn**
Product–design
& online shop
Germany
Hannes Beer
hannesbeer.de
2014

**290. Del Paso Blvd.**
**Partnership**
City management
USA
Mode Design
(Hans Bennewitz)
modedesign.us
2014

**291. The Image is Found**
Photography
USA
Go Forth Creative
goforthcreative.com
2014

289

290

291

292. **Flash Detergent for Grey London**
Detergent
United Kingdom
Rob Clarke Type Design & Lettering
robclarke.com
2006

293. **Flash Detergent for Grey London**
Detergent
United Kingdom
Rob Clarke Type Design & Lettering
robclarke.com
2006

294. **Razza**
Artisanal pizza restaurant
USA
The O Group
ogroup.net
2012

295. **Such & Such**
Online shop for designer products, accessories & homeware
United Kingdom
Bread Collective
breadcollective.co.uk
2013

292

293

294

295

**296. Bonbar**
Cocktail lounge & restaurant
United Kingdom
Precept
precept.co.uk
2013

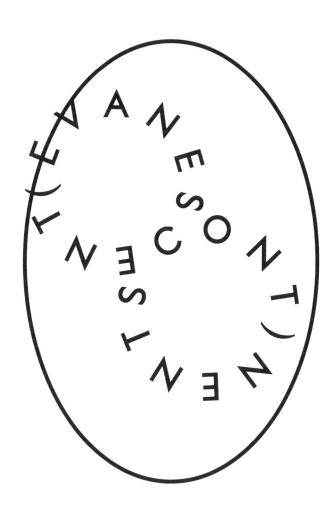

**297. Shoppinghour Magazine**
Art & philosophy magazine
United Kingdom
Think Work Observe
t-wo.it
2013

298               299

300               301

**298. Certus Consultores**
Financial, legal & accounting services
Mexico
Anagrama
anagrama.com
2013

**299. Buddhafields**
Holistic center & hotel
Mexico
Anagrama
anagrama.com
2014

**300. BRUNSWICKER studio**
Self-initiated
Denmark
BRUNSWICKER studio
brunswicker.dk
2011

**301. Løgismose**
Food, wine & delicacies
Denmark
Homework
homework.dk
2014

**302. Fonville Press**
Coastal bookstore
& coffee shop
USA
Slaughter Group
slaughtergroup.com

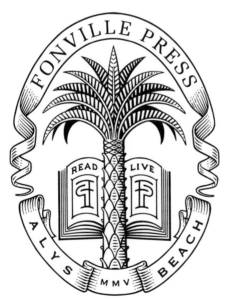

302

**303. East Beach**
New Urbanist community
USA
Slaughter Group
slaughtergroup.com

**304. Troy Rhone**
Garden design
USA
Slaughter Group
slaughtergroup.com

**305. Åbro Brewery**
Åbro is the oldest family
brewery in Sweden
Sweden
Bold
boldstockholm.se
2014

303

304

305

**306. Tucana Coffee**
Coffee shop
Canada
Doublenaut
doublenaut.com
2015

**307. Seafarers**
Hospitality
New Zealand
Inhouse
inhouse.nz
2013

**308. Bakery & Gourmet**
Restaurant
Brazil
P/P Studio
pedropaulino.com
2013

**309. Claridge's Hotel**
Luxury London hotel
United Kingdom
Peter Horridge
horridge.com
1996

**310. Sidra del Verano**
Cidery
Spain & Australia
Inhouse
inhouse.nz
2013

**311. Paris+Hendzel
Handcrafted Goods**
Production & sale of
handcrafted headwear
Poland
Paris+Hendzel Studio
parishendzelstudio.com
2014

309

310

311

**312. Great Western Building Tenants Co-Operation Housing Society Limited**
Housing society
India
Alok Nanda & Company
aloknanda.com
2012

**313. Harlem Haberdashery**
Fashion retailer & tailoring
USA
Amore Brand
Identity Studios
amore.se
2012

**314. Duncan Raban**
Photographer
United Kingdom
Peter Horridge
horridge.com
2011

**315. Demours Café Prive Select**
Purveyor of luxury coffee
USA
The O Group
ogroup.net
2014

**316. Allendale**
Mountain resort
South Africa
Monday Design
mondaydesign.co.za
2009

312

313

314

315

316

**317. The Americano**
Restaurant & bar
USA
J Fletcher Design
jfletcherdesign.com
2014

**318. Proper Baked Beans**
Proper's mission is to
reinstate baked beans as the
premium meal it once was
– how beans should always
have been
United Kingdom
Interabang
interabang.uk.com
2014

317

318

**319. Bettys**
Bakers, confectionery & tearooms
United Kingdom
Peter Horridge
horridge.com
2013

320

321

**320. Lloyds of London**
Banking & insurance
United Kingdom
Peter Horridge
horridge.com
2005

**321. British American
Household Staffing**
Household staffing solutions,
such as nannies, butlers,
chefs, chauffeurs & house
managers
USA
Knoed Creative
knoed.com
2012

**322. The Bishop of London
(currently Richard Chartres)**
Bishop of London
United Kingdom
Paperjam Design
paperjamdesign.com
2012

322

**323. Kuban Airways**
Airline
Russia
Peter Horridge
horridge.com
2010

**324. Hampstead**
New Urbanist community
USA
Slaughter Group
slaughtergroup.com

**325. Panesh & Accosiates**
Jurisprudence
Russia
Maksim Arbuzov
maksimarbuzov.com
2011

323

324

325

**326. Jacqueline Fleury**
Custom drapery
Canada
Sylvain Toulouse
sylvaintoulouse.com
2013

**327. New England
Shirt Company**
Shirt maker
USA
Slaughter Group
slaughtergroup.com

**328. The Shirt Factory**
Shirt maker
Sweden
Bold
boldstockholm.se
2013

327

328

**329. Steven Fox**
Exclusive retail jeweller
USA
Slaughter Group
slaughtergroup.com

**330. Beda Schmid**
Photographer
Switzerland
Studio Eusebio
studioeusebio.com
2013

**331. Chartered Institute
of Marketing**
International body for
marketing & business
development
United Kingdom
Rob Clarke Type Design
& Lettering/Brash Brands
robclarke.com
2014

329

330

331

**332. The Civil Service**
Government service
United Kingdom
Rob Clarke Type Design & Lettering/
35 Communications
robclarke.com
2009

333

334

335

336

337

**333. Bar Polski**
Bar
Poland
Dmowski & Co.
dmowski.co
2012

**334. Saiprezen FC**
Football team
Japan
Grand Deluxe
grand-deluxe.com
2011

**335. Egypt Lake
Trailbreakers**
Outdoor adventures
Canada
Chris Pecora Makes Stuff
chrispecora.com
2012

**336. Division of Labor**
Advertising agency
USA
Mikey Burton
mikeyburton.com
2010

**337. State of the Obvious®**
Merchandise
United Kingdom
Mash Creative
mashcreative.co.uk
2010

**338. Céltorony**
Gastro pub for kayakers,
canoers & rowers
Hungary
kissmiklos
kissmiklos.com
2015

**339. PJ's Bar and Grill**
Restaurant
United Kingdom
Mash Creative
mashcreative.co.uk
2012

338

339

**340. VIOLETA**
Bakers
Argentina
Anagrama
anagrama.com
2014

B E R     N Y C

**341. Benjamin Bojko**
Interface & software development
Germany
Ayaka Ito
ayakaito.com
2014

**342. Bulgarian State Archives**
Archives
Bulgaria
Stefan Kanchev
stefankanchev.com

**343. Union of the Bulgarian Philatelists**
Restaurant
Bulgaria
Stefan Kanchev
stefankanchev.com

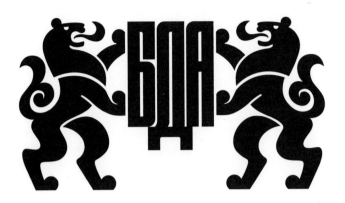

342

343

**344. Boyana Film Studios**
Studios
Bulgaria
Stefan Kanchev
stefankanchev.com

**345. Bulgarian Post**
Postal service
Bulgaria
Stefan Kanchev
stefankanchev.com

344

345

**346. Hungarian Coat of Arms**
Hungary
kissmiklos
kissmiklos.com
2013

347

348

349

350

351

352

353

**347. Gandour**
Food & confectionery
Lebanon
Mash Creative
mashcreative.co.uk
2014

**348. LV Field Day**
Local field day
USA
Greg Christman Design
gregchristmandesign.com
2015

**349. Frank Lantz**
Food & catering
Denmark
Homework
homework.dk
2013

**350. Theory11**
Playing card & magic
company
USA
The BlkSmith Co.
theblksmith.com
2014

**351. Testa Della Corsa**
Italian bike tours
United Kingdom
KVGD
kerrvernon.co.uk
2013

**352. Nike**
Multinational footwear
& apparel brand
USA
High Tide
hightide.nyc
2010

**353. Nike**
Multinational footwear
& apparel brand
USA
High Tide
hightide.nyc
2010

**354. National Museum of History**
Museum
Bulgaria
Stefan Kanchev
stefankanchev.com

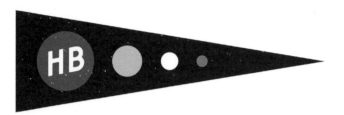

355

356          357

**355. Hannes Beer**
Graphic design & illustration
Germany
Hannes Beer
hannesbeer.de
2014

**356. Edelweiss Co.,Ltd.**
Western confectionery
Japan
UMA/design farm
umamu.jp
2014

**357. Ludwig Reiter**
Shoemaker
Austria
Golden Gate, commissioned
by Anzinger Wuenschner
Rasp
thegoldengate.eu
2008

**358. Soapy Joe's**
Garment care
USA
Brave UX
braveux.com
2014

358

**359. Sailing Team Gunilla**
**FIN-18**
Sports team
Finland
Ilkka Janatuinen
ilkkaj.com
2014

**360. Lord Smith Studio**
Graphic design studio
Spain
Eduardo Dosuá
eduardododosua.com
2012

**361. Esteban López**
Restaurant
Mexico
Firmalt
firmalt.com
2014

359

360

361

**362. AIGA Hawaii 5-O
Award Show**
AIGA's bi-annual graphic design
award show in Hawaii
USA
Wall-to-Wall Studios
walltowall.com
2013

**363. Gatley Festival**
Village festival event
United Kingdom
StudioDBD
studiodbd.com
2012

**364. Raina Knyaginya Panagyurishte**
Clothing, plastic & cardboard packs
Bulgaria
Stefan Kanchev
stefankanchev.com

**365. South Carolina**
**State Seal**
Self-initiated
USA
J Fletcher Design
jfletcherdesign.com
2014

**366. Peruvian government**
Self-initiated
Peru
IS Creative Studio
iscreativestudio.com
2014

365

366

**367. EIFA Parents**
The parents association
of 'London's premier
bilingual school' – L'Ecole
Internationale Franco–
Anglaise (EIFA)
United Kingdom
FL@33
flat33.com
2014

**368. Amatour**
Tennis tournament
Russia
Maksim Arbuzov
maksimarbuzov.com
2011

367

368

369

370

371

372

**369. Citizen Vintage**
Vintage clothing boutique
Canada
Michael Mason
mmason.ca
2014

**370. Sacramento Press**
Online newspaper
USA
Mode Design
(Hans Bennewitz) at Fuel
Creative Group
modedesign.us
fuelcreativegroup.com
2009

**371. The Chia Co's 'Australian
Open on Mulberry'**
Agriculture & food
Australia
DIA
dia.tv
2014

**372. NYTIMES**
Publishing
USA
Mother Design
motherdesign.com
derrickclee.com
Year 2010

**373. Bike Law**
Network of bicycle attorneys
USA
Fuzzco
fuzzco.com
2014

373

**374. Goodwater**
New Urbanist community
USA
Slaughter Group
slaughtergroup.com

**375. Bon Secour**
New Urbanist community
USA
Slaughter Group
slaughtergroup.com

374

375

376          377

**376. Körben**
Jewellery for cyclists
Hungary
kissmiklos
kissmiklos.com
2013

**377. Bienville Legacy**
Motorcycle design
USA
Eight Hour Day
eighthourday.com
2012

**378. Chateau Naftali**
High-end Kosher wine from
the Galilee in Israel
Israel
Yossi Belkin
yossigraphicdesign.com
2014

378

**379. Amaya Roasting Co.**
Coffee roasting
USA
Spindletop Design
spindletopdesign.com
2012

**380. Bikes on Wheels**
Bicycle retail & service
Canada
Doublenaut
doublenaut.com
2013

379

380

**Modern Heraldry: Volume 1**
Seals, Stamps, Crests & Shields

Edited and produced by Counter-Print.

**Design:** Jon Dowling & Céline Leterme
**Typefaces:** Druk and Moderat
**Printing and Binding:** 1010 Printing International Limited

**Publishing:** Counter-Print
counter-print.co.uk

First published in the United Kingdom in 2015 by Counter-Print,
reprinted in 2020.

©Counter-Print

**ISBN:** 978-0-9570816-7-3

**British Library cataloguing-in-publication data:** A catalogue
of this book can be found in the British Library.

With special thanks to all the contributors for their support, time and talent.